Veterinarian

Peggy J. Parks

KIDHAVEN
PRESS™

San Diego • Detroit • New York • San Francisco • Cleveland
New Haven, Conn. • Waterville, Maine • London • Munich

© 2004 by KidHaven Press. KidHaven Press is an imprint of The Gale Group, Inc., a division of Thomson Learning, Inc.

KidHaven™ and Thomson Learning™ are trademarks used herein under license.

For more information, contact
KidHaven Press
27500 Drake Rd.
Farmington Hills, MI 48331-3535
Or you can visit our Internet site at http://www.gale.com

LIBRARY OF CONGRESS CATALOGING-IN-PUBLICATION DATA

Parks, Peggy J., 1951–
  Veterinarian / by Peggy J. Parks.
    p. cm. — (Exploring Careers)
  Includes bibliographical references and index.
  Summary: Explores having a career as a veterinarian including the different kinds of veterinarians, their education and training, and where they work.
   ISBN 0-7377-2068-9
   1. Veterinarians—Juvenile literature. 2. Veterinary medicine—Vocational guidance—Unitged Stat ;—Juvenile literature. [1. Veterinarians. 2. Veterinary medicine—Vocational guidance. 3. Vocational guidance.] I. Title. II.
  Series: Exploring Careers (KidHaven Press)
   SF756.P27 2004
   636.089'069—dc22
                                                                2003027306

CONTENTS

From Parakeets to Palominos

Veterinarians are doctors whose patients are pets and wildlife. They perform many different services and may treat their patients at animal clinics, zoos, aquariums, or farms. In North America there are nearly seventy thousand practicing veterinarians.

Household Pet Doctors

Most veterinarians are general practitioners, which means they typically work with common pets such as dogs and cats. Many others also treat birds or small animals such as ferrets, guinea pigs, and hamsters. Dr. Rebecca Campbell is a general practitioner vet who owns Symphony Veterinary Center in New York City. One of her patients is a four-year-old Dalmatian named Oakley. During one visit, Dr. Campbell treated the dog because he had swallowed his ball. When she operated on him to remove it, she also found that he had swallowed a guitar string! Oakley did not learn his lesson, however. One month later he swallowed another ball and his owner again took him to the clinic. As Oakley shifted around in his cage, Dr. Campbell could hear the ball squeaking in the dog's stomach. She performed another operation to remove the ball, and Oakley recovered just fine.

A veterinarian tries to examine a wiggling puppy at an animal clinic. Most veterinarians work with common household pets.

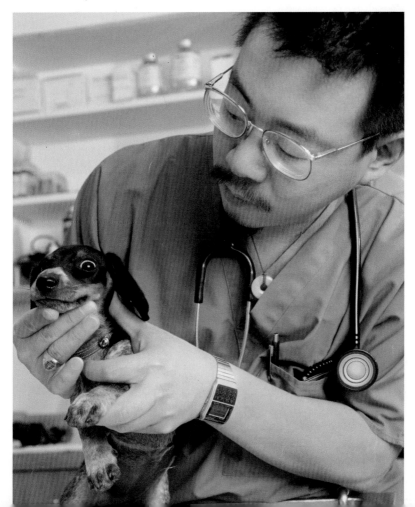

Veterinarians often work daytime hours, but many animal clinics also provide twenty-four-hour emergency care. Dr. Andy Sokol is an emergency vet who works at Grady Veterinary Hospital in Cincinnati. He sees pets of all shapes and sizes, and he has treated everything from broken bones to breathing problems. Many of his cases involve dogs that swallow objects such as bones, balls, and gobs of string. Dr. Sokol has also treated dogs that have eaten Christmas tinsel, screwdrivers, socks, blankets, and entire loaves of bread.

Exotic Pet Vets

Some veterinarians specialize in pets that slither, scamper, or hop. Dr. Gregory Mertz, who has a Massachusetts practice called the Odd Pet Vet, specializes in exotic pets such as snakes. He also treats iguanas and shiny lizards called **skinks**, as well as a variety of spiders, turtles, rodents—even alligators. One of his patients is a yellow and white, seven-foot-long python named Slick. During one visit Dr. Mertz treated the fifteen-pound snake for a respiratory infection. On a different occasion he performed surgery on a python that had eaten a pair of its owner's underwear.

Because of his unique specialty, Dr. Mertz is always prepared to face the unexpected. One man brought in his tarantula because it lost a leg when a book fell on it. Another brought in a pet daddy

Some veterinarians specialize in treating exotic pets like snakes, iguanas, and lizards.

longlegs spider that was infested with mites. Dr. Mertz has treated turtles with mouth sores, salamanders with infections, and iguanas refusing to eat. A panicked woman brought in her son's frog after she had accidentally washed it in the washing machine. To the mother's relief, Dr. Mertz was able to treat the frog, and she took it back home.

Down on the Farm

Just as people depend on veterinarians to take care of their pets, farmers depend on them to keep their farm animals healthy. These doctors are often called large-animal specialists or livestock vets. They travel to farms and ranches to care for horses, cows, pigs, goats, sheep, and other animals. Their visits may be routine, or they may provide emergency treatment.

Dr. Janice Posnikoff is an **equine veterinarian**, which means she specializes in treating horses. As a young teenager she had a horse named Beauty. The horse developed a life-threatening leg disease, and a veterinarian saved its life. After that experience Dr. Posnikoff decided to become a veterinarian. Today she operates a mobile clinic in California and drives from stable to stable to treat her equine patients. She says the best thing about being a veterinarian is seeing the results of a job well done: "Surgeries that go off without a hitch, watching a once-lame horse trotting around. . . and foals that are born healthy and happy. Think-

An equine veterinarian files down a horse's chipped tooth. Veterinarians who work with large animals may also be called livestock vets.

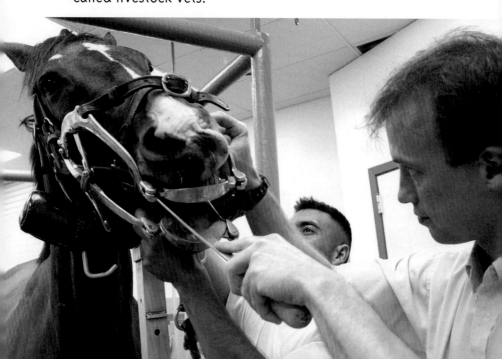

ing about the thank you cards and pictures my clients send me brings a tear to my eye."[1]

Cages and Fish Tanks

Another type of large-animal veterinarian is one who treats zoo animals. Zoo veterinarians treat elephants, rhinoceroses, giraffes, tigers, lions, and all the other wild animals that live in zoos. Dr. Jim Rasmussen, a veterinarian at the Minnesota Zoo, is known as "Dr. Zoolittle." He has treated snapping turtles, grizzly bears, and dog-sized, South American rodents called **pacas**. One time Dr. Rasmussen needed to remove a stuffed animal from the stomach of a **Komodo dragon** named Doni. A child visiting the zoo had accidentally dropped her toy cat into Doni's cage, and the huge reptile swallowed it.

Zoo animals do not necessarily cooperate when they need medical treatment. Often they get angry with the veterinarians who examine them and remember their anger for a very long time. According to Dr. Mary Denver, a zoo veterinarian in Baltimore, a polar bear held a longtime grudge against her. She once checked the animal because it had a mark on its nose. It did not appreciate the examination. Ever since, whenever the bear sees Dr. Denver, it starts jumping up and down on two legs as it spits, drools, and growls.

Aquariums also need veterinarians to take care of fish and other aquatic creatures. One example is

Boston's New England Aquarium. It is home to more than seven thousand varieties of aquatic wildlife such as fish, penguins, seals, sharks, and sea turtles. Veterinarians who work for the aquarium's medical center specialize in aquatic wildlife, and they care for all the aquarium animals. They also treat sick or injured creatures that have been rescued. One of their patients was a young male seal named Barney that was stranded on the beach. He suffered from bite wounds on his flippers and an infection of his gums. As soon as Barney had recovered, he was released back into the ocean.

Animal Specialists

Just like doctors for humans, some veterinarians specialize in a particular area of medicine. For instance, those who specialize in allergies and skin diseases are called **veterinary dermatologists**. **Veterinary oncologists** specialize in cancerous growths. Veterinary surgeons perform many types of surgical operations, and **veterinary cardiologists** focus on heart problems. There are also veterinary dentists who care for animals' teeth and gums.

To treat animals suffering from eye problems, there are **veterinary ophthalmologists**. One of these specialists, Dr. Sam Vainisi from Wisconsin, has performed eye surgery on a nine-thousand-pound elephant, a Siberian tiger, a horned owl, an orangutan, and a large, slow-moving mammal called a **three-toed sloth**.

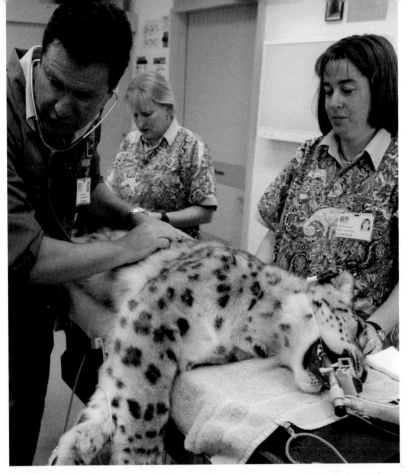

A zoo veterinarian and his staff perform an exam on a snow leopard. Some animals need to be sedated before they can be examined.

Veterinarians may treat dogs and cats, or large wild animals such as elephants, giraffes, and bears. They may care for livestock on a farm, or treat fish and other creatures that live in aquariums. Whatever their specialty, and no matter if their patients bark, whinny, scamper, slither, or swim, all veterinarians are important. Anyone who loves a pet, owns a farm, or loves nature and wildlife, depends on the valuable health-care services that these professionals provide.

CHAPTER 2

What It Takes to Be a Veterinarian

Many veterinarians say they decided what career to pursue at a very young age. In most cases, it was because they loved animals. Yet even though this is an important quality for veterinarians, there is much more to it than that. The road to a career in veterinary medicine is long and difficult, and involves years of college study, hands-on training, and hard work.

An Early Start

Young people interested in veterinary careers often start preparing while they are still in high school. That is because the college classes that veterinary students need are very heavy in science and math. High school students who take chemistry, biology, physics, and calculus, as well as other science and math courses, will have an easier time in college. Also, by taking these classes they are more likely to be accepted into the college of their choice.

Another way young people prepare for veterinary careers is to volunteer or work part-time at animal clinics, zoos, farms, animal shelters, or wildlife parks. When Dr. Posnikoff was in high school she worked part-time for the veterinarian who saved her horse's life. Later, because of her interest in horses, she worked at a horse-racing track. She offers this advice for young people interested in veterinary careers: "Work hard at school and get good grades. . . . Get lots of experience with animals. Really be sure that veterinary medicine is your calling."[2]

A career in veterinary medicine requires years of study, and many students get jobs with animal clinics, wildlife parks, or farms to give them hands-on experience.

Preprofessional Study

To become veterinarians, high school graduates must attend a four-year college or university before being admitted to veterinary school. During their undergraduate college years, preveterinary students may choose their own major. According to the North Carolina State College of Veterinary Medicine, one of the top veterinary schools in the United States, five majors are most common for aspiring veterinarians. These are animal science, poultry science, **zoology** (the study of animals), biology, **biochemistry** (the chemistry of living things), and **microbiology** (the study of living organisms that can be seen only under a microscope). Although most students who are admitted to veterinary school have earned a bachelor's degree, this is not always a requirement. However, these schools require students to complete a number of specialized college classes, which usually takes about three years.

There are less than thirty-five veterinary schools in North America and a limited amount of openings for new students—which means being accepted into veterinary school is highly competitive. When considering applicants, the schools evaluate such factors as grade average, college curriculum, experience with animals, and entrance examination scores.

Four Intense Years

Once students are accepted into veterinary school, they have a tough road ahead of them. Dr. Pos-

A student studies the anatomy of a bird in zoology class. Besides zoology, students may major in animal science, biochemistry, microbiology, biology, or poultry science.

nikoff explains: "Four years sounds like a long time, but it goes by so quickly and there is so much to learn. I wish I could go back to school and take those classes again . . . I would probably listen a whole lot better!"[3]

Most veterinary programs are divided into two phases. The first phase is academic and involves two years of intense science-related study. Students take classes in **anatomy**, **physiology**, **pathology**, **pharmacology**, and microbiology. Much of their time is spent in classrooms and in college laboratories. In addition they must spend many hours on library research, reading assignments, and studying for exams. Because of the heavy workload, it is common for veterinary students to work and study at all hours of the day and night, including weekends.

The second half of veterinary school is the clinical phase. Students continue attending classes to learn about animal diseases, surgery, and other science and medical subjects. They also begin to apply what they have learned by working in an animal hospital or clinic. Most veterinary schools have teaching hospitals right on their campuses.

Cats lie and walk about a classroom, while veterinary students use them to make the practice "rounds."

These are actual clinics where people can take their pets for treatment. Under the supervision of instructors (who are also licensed veterinarians), students gain hands-on experience with animals. They learn how to give examinations, diagnose and treat diseases and injuries, and perform surgery.

The Fourth Year and Beyond

During the fourth year, students do clinical rotations, which allows them to work with many different types of veterinarians. They may observe and assist veterinary surgeons, dermatologists, oncologists, and ophthalmologists, as well as other specialists. Students also experience veterinary specialties such as aquatic medicine, exotic-animal medicine, and zoo-animal medicine. In most cases veterinary students are not required to complete an internship during their college training. However, many choose to do so anyway to gain valuable work experience. Students who want to specialize in a particular type of animal or area of medicine must usually complete a one-year internship after veterinary school.

Before graduates can practice veterinary medicine, they must get a license from the state in which they plan to work. This certifies them as a doctor of veterinary medicine, or DVM. Then they may set up their own practice or join a practice with other veterinarians. Yet even though they

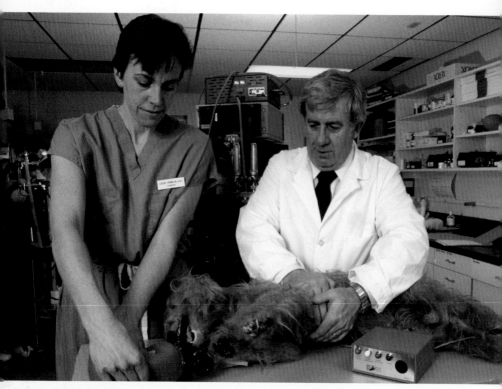

A veterinary student (left) practices resuscitating a dummy dog. Students sometimes practice with dummies to avoid mistakenly injuring a real animal.

have finished school, their education does not end. To keep up with the latest knowledge and technology, veterinarians must read scientific journals and participate in professional seminars and workshops. Also, many states require them to attend education courses to keep their veterinary licenses current.

The Right Stuff

Students who make it through veterinary school know how much work is involved in being a veterinarian. But along with the willingness to work hard, there are certain personal qualities veterinarians need. They must have confidence in themselves, and be able to think quickly, solve problems, and make decisions. Also, along with caring deeply about animals, they must be able to work well with people. They need excellent communication skills, including the ability to listen well.

One essential quality for veterinarians is the ability to cope with difficult situations. No matter

A fourth-year student (left) holds a clouded leopard cub while a zoo veterinarian takes the cub's temperature.

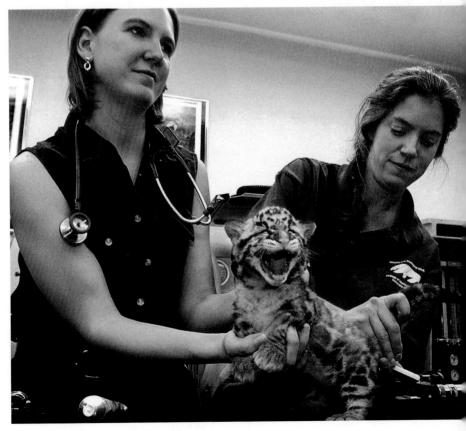

how skilled they may be, there are times when they cannot save an animal that is seriously injured or sick. There are also times when it is necessary to **euthanize** an animal, or put it to sleep. Most veterinarians say that is the most difficult part of their jobs. Even though an animal may be suffering from disease or injury, they still feel sorrow for having to take its life. If the animal is someone's beloved pet, veterinarians must be sensitive to the owner's grief.

Not everyone is cut out for a career in veterinary medicine. Even people who have a deep affection for animals may not want to become animal doctors. However, for those who have the right personal qualities—and the willingness to spend years, energy, and money to be educated and trained—becoming a veterinarian is the best possible choice they could make.

CHAPTER 3

In the Clinic and at the Zoo

Depending on their specialties, veterinarians' jobs often differ from day to day. They perform regular checkups, give shots, clean animals' teeth, and prescribe medicines. They are also called during emergencies when pets are sick or injured. Sometimes veterinarians care for female pets throughout a pregnancy, and then deliver their babies. Depending on what types of animals are treated, and what they are treated for, veterinarians' days can vary from slow to hectic, and from ordinary to strange.

A Day in the Clinic

Dr. Coretta Patterson is a veterinarian at the University of Georgia's veterinary teaching hospital. She regularly treats dogs and cats in the pet clinic.

One day she examined Danté and Beanie, two country cats that spent most of their time outside. The cats had not visited a vet for three years, so Dr. Patterson spent quite a bit of time examining them. She weighed them and checked their **vital signs**, including heart rate, breathing, temperature, and blood pressure. She closely checked their fur to make sure they did not have fleas. She felt through their skin to check their kidneys, liver, intestines, and heart. Then she used a needle to draw blood from each cat, to test it for **feline leukemia**. Dr. Patterson finished the exam by giving both Danté and Beanie shots to protect against

A veterinary student assists a veterinarian during an examination of an English springer spaniel. Veterinarians who work in animal clinics typically treat dogs and cats the most.

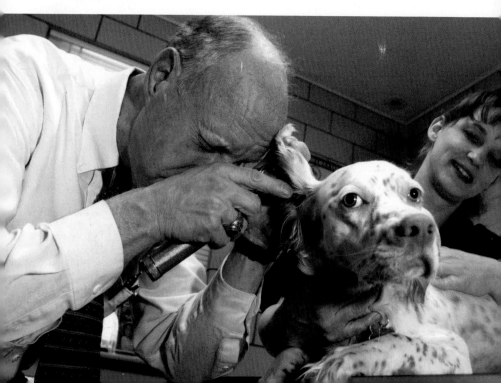

rabies and other diseases. Then she met with their owner to give a report of the exams.

Next Dr. Patterson examined Chip, a thirteen-year-old English springer spaniel. From previous experience she knew that Chip did not like going to the vet, so she carefully put a muzzle on his mouth. This would protect her if he got scared and decided to bite. Chip's owner had taken him to the clinic because the dog's ears were bothering him. Dr. Patterson examined Chip and found that he had an ear infection. She thoroughly cleaned his ears and applied some medicine.

These types of routine examinations and treatments are typical for Dr. Patterson, who works during the day from Monday through Friday. In addition to her veterinary work, she teaches students in the classroom and in the clinic. She also regularly meets with students who need help or advice.

A Night in the ER

Veterinarian Andy Sokol's schedule is very different from Dr. Patterson's. Dr. Sokol works from 7:00 P.M. to 7:00 A.M., which he prefers because he says nighttime is when the most interesting cases come into the clinic. One night he treated a female boxer named Angel that had been shot through the nose. He patched the wound and gave Angel some medicine to stop the spread of infection. His next case was a Siberian husky named Snow that

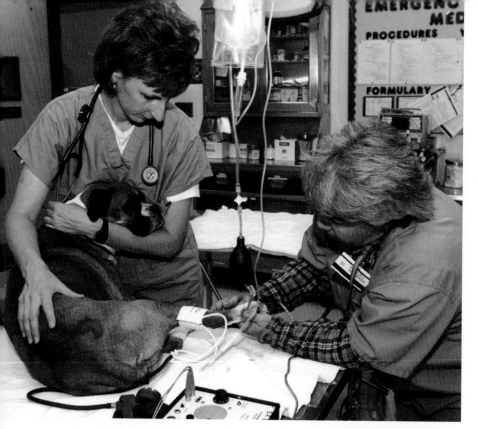

A veterinarian checks a boxer's blood pressure in a pet emergency room. Veterinarians who work in emergency rooms usually treat injured animals.

had eaten some of his owner's muscle relaxant pills. The pills were safe for humans but could be fatal to animals. Dr. Sokol gave Snow some medicine that would cause him to vomit the drugs. He also inserted an **intravenous catheter (IV)** into the dog's vein so medicine could quickly be carried into his system.

Later that night Dr. Sokol examined a police dog with a wounded paw. He gave the dog **anesthesia** to make him sleep, and then sewed up his wound. He also treated a Labrador retriever with a bad cut on his ear, and a cat that was injured when a car backed over it. In all these cases Dr. Sokol was able to treat the animals and send them home.

Life as a Zoo Doctor

Unlike dogs, cats, and other household pets, zoo animals cannot be loaded into a car and driven to a clinic. Veterinarians must treat them at the zoos where they live. Dr. Steven Marks, a veterinarian from Pittsburgh, specializes in caring for animals in zoos and aquariums. He has performed such jobs as removing an infected tusk from an elephant, operating on a reindeer with a **hernia**, stitching the cut ear of a **lemur**, and treating a monkey for malnutrition.

A San Diego Zoo veterinarian tries to get a look at this giant panda cub's teeth during a routine examination.

One of Dr. Marks's days involved treating a giant sea turtle that had sores on its shell called **lesions**. With the assistance of the zookeeper, Dr. Marks lifted the turtle from its tank and lowered it to the ground so he could examine it. He scraped the infected area on the shell and covered it with a medicine patch, which he attached with a thick coating of waterproof paste. His veterinary assistant used a hair dryer to dry the paste, and the turtle was put back into the tank.

Dr. Marks next performed a physical on Chuckles, an Amazon River dolphin. The zoo curator loaded Chuckles onto a specially designed stretcher with holes for his flippers, and put a strap around his mouth to keep him from biting. Then the stretcher (with Chuckles inside) was hung on a scale so the dolphin's weight could be recorded. Dr. Marks drew a blood sample, which he says is tricky with dolphins because their veins are hard to find. Once he had finished drawing blood, he cleaned Chuckles's teeth. The last step was to scrub him with an antibacterial solution to guard against the fungus that grows in water tanks. After his exam Dr. Marks determined that Chuckles was in good health, and the dolphin was returned to his tank.

Creatures in the Wild

Some veterinarians specialize in wild animals that are not in captivity. Dr. Kathleen Ramsay became

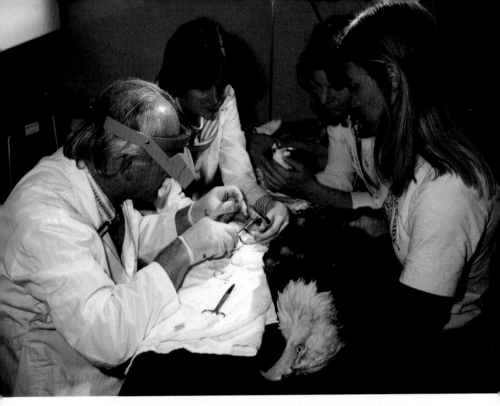

A veterinarian operates on a bald eagle's injured foot.
Some veterinarians specialize in treating wild animals.

interested in wildlife medicine when she was a veterinary student and a golden eagle was brought to
the clinic where she worked. The eagle's legs were
caught in a steel trap, and the bird was near death.
Ramsay vowed to nurse the eagle back to health—
and that is exactly what she did. From that point on
she was committed to helping save wild animals
and birds. In 1986 she founded a clinic in Espanola,
New Mexico, called the Wildlife Center. Today
people from all over the country take sick and injured creatures to Dr. Ramsay, who has become a
well-known veterinarian and surgeon.

Dr. Ramsay's schedule is always hectic. During
one day she treated a horned owl that had been

shot and a hawk recovering from a leg fracture. She bandaged sores on the feet of two golden eagles and examined a fawn that hikers had brought to the clinic. When three angry and snarling baby raccoons were brought in, Dr. Ramsay diagnosed them with a deadly virus called **distemper**. Wearing rubber gloves to protect herself from being scratched or bitten, she gave them shots to get rid of the virus. Then she used a tongue depressor to feed them baby food. With these and other animals Dr. Ramsay sees, her goal is to help them become healthy so she can release them back into their natural habitats.

Veterinarians may spend days examining dogs, cats, eagles, or hawks, or nights treating injured snakes and lizards. They may work in clinics or treat animals in zoos and aquariums. Their jobs and schedules depend on when they work, where they practice, and what they specialize in. No two veterinarians do exactly the same thing, but there is a common thread that ties them all together: their commitment to keeping animals healthy.

CHAPTER 4

Meet a Veterinarian

Dr. Holly Knor decided to become a veterinarian when she was just five years old. Her parents bought her a toy poodle, which she named Pepi. From that point on she was an animal lover. "Having my own dog nourished my love of animals," she says. "I didn't even know what veterinarians were until I got Pepi. But after one trip to the vet's office, I was hooked. I knew I would become a veterinarian someday. Actually, I believe that was God's plan for me."[4] Today, Dr. Knor works for Alameda East Veterinary Hospital in Denver, Colorado, where she has been since 1995. She is a well-known veterinarian —not only in Denver, but throughout the country— because she is also a television star. Dr. Knor is one of the veterinarians featured on the Animal Planet series, *Emergency Vets*.

Caring for family pets can lead to an interest in veterinary sciences.

An Early Start

When Dr. Knor was a young teenager in Fort Lauderdale, Florida, she started working part-time for Dr. L.W. George, her family veterinarian. She was so eager to be around the animals that she begged him to let her work at his clinic. "I spent all my spare time there," she says, "including after school, holidays, and weekends. I loved the work so much, I just couldn't get enough of it. I cleaned cages and kennels, washed syringes, and did anything else Dr. George needed me to do. Every once in a while, if I was really lucky, he would let me assist him with a patient. That's when I learned a lot about animal behaviors. When animals pin their ears back, wag their tails, or have their backs up in the air, they're sending messages. If you observe them enough, and pay attention, you will begin to see what they are trying to tell you."

Dr. Knor worked at the clinic until she was sixteen, and then she went to New Zealand to be an exchange student. She says she gained even more knowledge about animals from that experience: "I spent some time on a sheep ranch, which was neat because it gave me a chance to observe larger animals. One day I was out running and found a lamb with its neck caught under a fence. There was no one to help me so I picked it up—it weighed about forty pounds—and I ran two miles back to the farmhouse with the lamb in my arms. Unfortunately the little thing didn't survive because its injuries were too severe. But that experience was valuable to me. The people did their best to help the lamb, and it showed me how farmers took care of their own animals."

College and Beyond

Dr. Knor returned to Fort Lauderdale, and after graduating from high school, she enrolled in a community college. She attended for two years and also worked for Dr. George as a veterinary assistant and receptionist. After earning her associate's degree she transferred to Colorado State University, where she earned her bachelor of science in microbiology. She applied to Colorado State's veterinary school and was accepted.

In 1995, during Dr. Knor's last year of veterinary school, she applied for an internship at Alameda East. She got the position and spent the next year working long hours for minimal pay. But she says the valuable experience she gained was well worth it. When the year was up she was asked to stay as a staff veterinarian, and she took the job.

Never a Dull Moment

Dr. Knor is a general practitioner, so most of her patients are household pets such as dogs and cats. But she says she has also seen some unusual animals: "I was once on emergency duty, and a woman brought in her pet **hedgehog** that had just

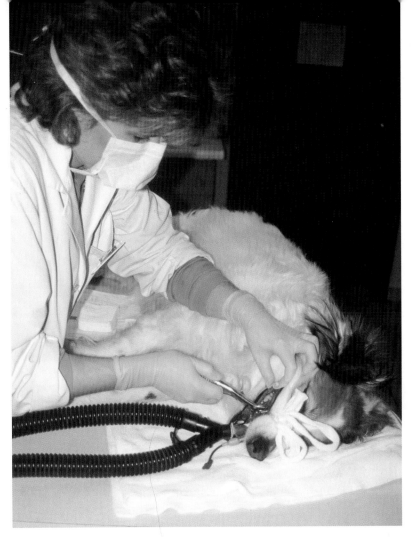

A veterinary student works on a patient. When Dr. Knor was a student, she worked as a veterinary assistant and then as an intern to gain hands-on experience.

delivered three babies. She would not nurse the babies, so the owner was concerned that the hedgehog might have an infection in her **mammary glands**. For anyone who isn't familiar with hedgehogs, they are tiny animals that fit in the palm of your hand, and they have poky spines all over their bodies. Whenever you handle them, they curl up in a ball to protect themselves. The only way I could examine the mama was to give her anesthesia so she would open up. And the only way I could check her mammary glands was to see if they produced milk. Now, lots of people can say they've milked a cow but I can truthfully say that I have milked a hedgehog! Incidentally, everything turned out okay, and Mrs. Hedgehog nursed her babies just fine."

Working with unusual animals presents unique challenges for a veterinarian. Dr. Knor's most unusual patient was a hedgehog like this one.

Another of Dr. Knor's unusual cases also involved a small pet. "A lady brought her hamster in because it had a tumor. I had to do surgery to remove the tumor, and then send it to the lab for testing. By the time we were done, the lady's bill was something like $350 for the hamster's emergency care. Some people would balk at spending that kind of money on such a tiny animal, but the lady told me, 'This is my pet and I love it. I have to give it the care it needs.' Things like that make me realize that people love their pets unconditionally, and that love is not dependent on whether the pets are small or large."

Ouch!

When asked if she has ever been bitten by one of her patients, Dr. Knor says yes—and it was a dangerous experience. "A stray cat was brought in that had been hit by a car. It wasn't responsive at all, and in cases like that one of the first things we assume is that the animal is in shock. We test for that by looking at its gums, so I lifted up the cat's lip—and suddenly she came alive! She clamped down on the middle finger of my right hand and bit through my fingernail. The nurses had to pry her jaws apart to get her teeth off my finger. Cats have very dirty mouths so I immediately started taking antibiotics, but thirty-six hours later my finger was obviously infected and the pain was unbearable—even pain medication didn't help. I went to the emergency room and the doctor told me, 'You need surgery *now!'* The infection was so severe he said he would be lucky to save my hand. Fortunately, I only lost the tip of my finger, but I was out of work for a month. Most people don't realize that when they are bitten by an animal, they must get emergency treatment immediately. Being bitten can be a life-threatening situation."

Life as a TV Star

When Dr. Knor decided to become a veterinarian, she had no idea she would someday end up on television. "I went to school to become a vet, and never dreamed I'd be on a successful TV show! It's a privilege to be able to do that." She has traveled all over the country with Animal Planet and has even appeared on *The Oprah Winfrey Show*. She says people often recognize her and sometimes ask for her autograph.

Dr. Knor says that being on *Emergency Vets* has given her opportunities to educate the public about veterinary medicine. "There is a misconception that veterinarians just give vaccines and shoot animals when they have broken legs. Some people have no idea what we really do, and this show allows us to increase awareness about animals and things that pet owners should know. For instance, I once did a show that featured a particular kind of treatment. Later I was at an Animal Planet expo in Indianapolis and a lady came up to me and said, 'You have to meet my dog; she's alive because of you.' She wanted to personally thank me, and it was heartwarming."

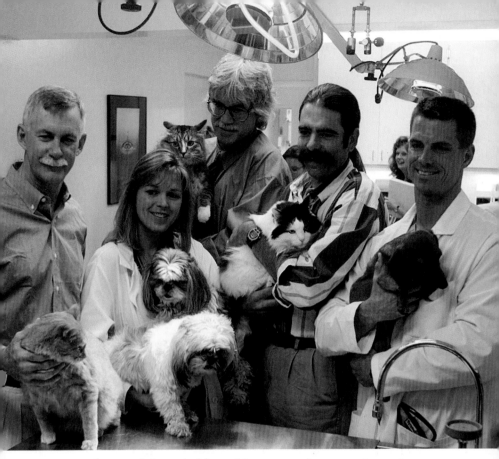

Dr. Knor (second from left) and her coworkers at Alameda East Veterinary Hospital in Denver, Colorado, star on the television show *Emergency Vets* on Animal Planet.

Message to Aspiring Vets

Dr. Knor says that being a veterinarian is both rewarding and fulfilling, and she recommends it for the right person. "It requires an amazing amount of patience, dedication, and hard work . . . but if it is in your heart to do this, I would definitely encourage you to give it all you've got. I've known I would be a veterinarian since I was very young. And I wouldn't change one thing about what I have done with my life."

NOTES

Chapter 1: From Parakeets to Palominos

1. Quoted in "I'm an Equine Veterinarian," *Young Rider,* July/August 2001, p. 28.

Chapter 2: What It Takes to Be a Veterinarian

2. Quoted in "I'm an Equine Veterinarian," p. 28.

3. Quoted in "I'm an Equine Veterinarian," p. 28.

Chapter 4: Meet a Veterinarian

4. All quotes in Chapter 4: Dr. Holly Knor, interview with author, October 2, 2003.

GLOSSARY

anatomy: The science of body structure.

anesthesia: Medication that reduces feeling or causes a patient to fall asleep.

biochemistry: The study of the chemistry of living things.

distemper: An infectious and deadly viral disease.

equine veterinarian: A veterinarian who specializes in the treatment of horses.

euthanize: To end an animal's life, usually by an injection.

feline leukemia: A deadly virus that is specific to cats.

hedgehog: A small, spiny animal that rolls into a ball for protection.

hernia: A bulge caused by a weak area or tear in the muscle.

intravenous catheter (IV): A device used so that drugs can be injected directly into a vein.

Komodo dragon: The largest lizard in the world, which can grow to be up to ten feet long.

lemur: A furry creature in the same family as monkeys and apes.

lesion: An area that is injured or diseased (such as a sore or blister).

mammary gland: A milk-producing gland in female mammals.

microbiology: The study of living organisms that are visible only under a microscope.

paca: A dog-sized rodent that lives in tropical climates.

pathology: The study of disease.

pharmacology: The study of drugs and their effects.

physiology: The study of how the body works.

skink: A smooth, shiny lizard.

three-toed sloth: A slow-moving mammal with long hooklike claws.

veterinary cardiologist: A veterinarian who specializes in animal heart problems.

veterinary dermatologist: A veterinarian who specializes in allergies and diseases of the skin.

veterinary oncologist: A veterinarian who specializes in cancerous growths.

veterinary ophthalmologist: A veterinarian who specializes in eye diseases and eye surgery.

vital signs: The signs of life, such as pulse, breathing, blood pressure, and temperature.

zoology: The study of animals.

Books

Mary Bowman-Kruhm, *A Day in the Life of a Veterinarian.* New York: PowerKids Press, 1999. Readers will travel along with a veterinarian as she makes house calls to visit a variety of different animals.

Jennifer Owings Dewey, *Wildlife Rescue: The Work of Dr. Kathleen Ramsay.* Honesdale, PA: Boyds Mills Press, 1994. The story of a veterinarian who founded New Mexico's Wildlife Center, which treats sick and injured birds, and animals from all over the western United States.

Jean L. Patrick, *Cows, Cats, and Kids: A Veterinarian's Family at Work.* Honesdale, PA: Boyds Mills Press, 2003. The story of a rural South Dakota veterinarian who works with all sizes and types of animals, often with his wife and three children working alongside him.

Willow Ann Sirch, *Careers with Animals: The Humane Society of the United States.* Golden, CO: Fulcrum, 2000. Describes careers in veterinary medicine, as well as other related jobs for kids who love domestic animals and wildlife.

Periodicals

Lynn Coulter, "Wet Vet," *Ranger Rick,* April 1998. The story of Dr. Chris Keller, a veterinarian whose patients are the fish, alligators, ducks, frogs, and other creatures that live at the Tennessee Aquarium.

Nancy Dreschel, "Scooter's Story," *Jack and Jill,* September 2000. An article written by a veterinarian from Pennsylvania who describes her treatment of a seriously injured beagle puppy.

Mark Wheeler, "All Creatures Great and Odd," *Discover,* December 1997. A fascinating article about veterinarians who specialize in treating exotic pets such as tarantulas, pythons, and turtles.

Geoff Williams, "Animal ER," *Boys' Life,* November 1998. Gives readers a firsthand glimpse at Grady Veterinary Hospital in Cincinnati, Ohio, which has a twenty-four-hour emergency room.

Web Sites

American Veterinary Medical Association (www. avma.org). An informative site about veterinary careers that has a special section designed just for kids.

Animal Doc Com (www.uga.edu). This site, maintained by the University of Georgia's College of Veterinary Medicine, was created especially for kids interested in veterinary careers. Includes information about a variety of animals, a "Meet the Doctor" section, and a virtual tour of the college.

Animal Planet (www.animalplanet.com). Includes a section entitled *Emergency Vets,* which introduces Dr. Holly Knor and the other stars of the hit television show by the same name. Also includes a number of stories featuring unusual situations faced by the vets.

INDEX

ABOUT THE AUTHOR

Peggy J. Parks holds a bachelor of science degree from Aquinas College in Grand Rapids, Michigan, where she graduated magna cum laude. She is a freelance writer who has written more than twenty-five books for Gale Group imprints, including Blackbirch Press, KidHaven Press, and Lucent Books. Parks lives in Muskegon, Michigan, a town she says inspires her writing because of its location on the shores of Lake Michigan.